Adventures with Natural Wonders

Edited by

Karen Kwek

 **WS Education**

NEW JERSEY · LONDON · SINGAPORE · BEIJING · SHANGHAI · HONG KONG · TAIPEI · CHENNAI · TOKYO

Published by

WS Education, an imprint of

World Scientific Publishing Co. Pte. Ltd.

5 Toh Tuck Link, Singapore 596224

USA office: 27 Warren Street, Suite 401-402, Hackensack, NJ 07601

UK office: 57 Shelton Street, Covent Garden, London WC2H 9HE

National Library Board, Singapore Cataloguing in Publication Data
Name(s): Kwek, Karen, editor.
Title: Adventures with natural wonders / edited by Karen Kwek.
Other title(s): World of science comics ; 10.
Description: Singapore : WS Education : English Corner Publishing Pte Ltd, [2022]
Identifier(s): OCN 1261878496 | ISBN 978-981-124-171-0 (hardcover) | ISBN 978-981-124-191-8 (paperback) |
    978-981-124-172-7 (ebook for institutions) | 978-981-124-173-4 (ebook for individuals)
Subject(s): LCSH: Natural history--Comic books, strips, etc. | Natural history--Juvenile literature. |
    Natural areas--Comic books, strips, etc. | Natural areas--Behavior--Juvenile literature. | Graphic novels.
Classification: DDC 508--dc23

British Library Cataloguing-in-Publication Data
A catalogue record for this book is available from the British Library.

Published by arrangement by ENGLISH CORNER PUBLISHING PTE LTD

Design and layout: Loo Chuan Ming

Printed in Singapore

What are natural wonders?

If you said something like "amazing effects in nature", well done! But natural wonders also include instances where human activity assists in the creation of something wonderful, such as the world's largest big cat!

Where are the most impressive waterfalls on Earth? What makes the oceans glow in the dark? See Cappadocia from a hot-air balloon. Walk in the footprints of mythical giants. From coloured sand to mysterious clouds, experience phenomena in nature that will make you go "wow"!

Experience a world of
interactive discoveries!

 Scan to watch a video on activating AR in 3 easy steps.

1

Download the SnapLearn app.

2

Activate by scanning this book's barcode. Then, tap on the book cover image on your screen.

3

Wherever you see this icon, scan the whole page.

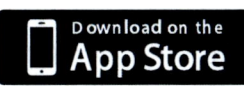 

SnapLearn is compatible with devices running minimally on iOS 8 and Android 5.0 with gyroscope. For the best AR experience, please scan the physical or PDF version of the book. For any app-related issues, please contact us via email at hello@snaplearn.com.

Powered By :

Contents

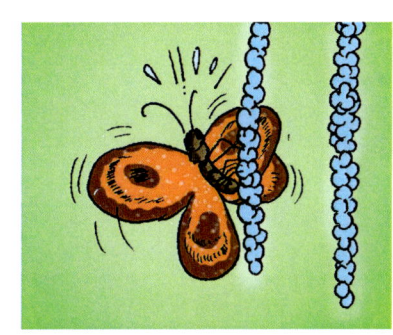

Wild River Adventures

Knowbot and Bobo explore the Amazon River…

Wow, Knowbot, look! The river is teeming with fish!

Yes, did you know that more than 3,000 species of fish live in the Amazon River?

Click...

Oh, really? Wow!

Splash!

This one looks like a dolphin!

Ha ha, that's because it's an Amazon river dolphin — but dolphins are mammals, not fish.

It seems very friendly! I'd love to play with it!

I don't think you can do that! There are frightful piranhas in the Amazon River.

Yikes! Piranhas!

I'd be eaten alive! I don't want to swim in this river!

Bobo, you made the right decision.

Wild River Adventures

Knowbot, which way are we going now?

I'm not sure. Let me check my map.

Humpf... I think we should go...

Mighty Amazon

The Amazon River winds through northern South America, beginning in the Andes Mountains and emptying into the Atlantic Ocean. More than 6,000 kilometres long, it boasts the largest water flow and catchment area, and the most number of tributaries of all the rivers in the world.

Huh? What?

Quick, we have to get that map back or we'll get lost on the Amazon River!

Hey! The monkey took my map!

Eek... Eek...

Oh no! Don't you have a map in that computer brain of yours?

No, because I can't get a strong data signal here! We must find that cheeky monkey!

Nghh...

Oh! It is trapped!

It needs our help!

Screech... Screech... Screech...

A River Runs Through It

Most of the Amazon River runs through Peru and Brazil, but its tributaries also cross parts of Colombia, Ecuador, Venezuela, Bolivia, Suriname, Guyana and French Guiana. That's nine countries!

Ha ha... We have a good catch, a squirrel monkey!

What did I tell you? This rainforest is going to make us rich. It's full of rare specimens that people will pay big money to buy!

Screech...

Screech...

We are going to catch more amazing animals here!

Yes, Jim!

Screech...

Screech...

Oh no!

They are poachers! They catch and sell animals illegally!

Knowbot! Will they hunt that friendly Amazon river dolphin?

Huh? I hope not!

We must do something to stop them!

Yes! I have an idea!

Bad Reputation

The red-bellied piranha (*Pygocentrus nattereri*) is one of many popular aquarium fish that are native to the Amazon River. Despite its reputation as a ferocious predator, the red-bellied piranha rarely attacks humans. Red-bellied piranhas have been known to feed on the carcasses of birds and capybaras, but they typically eat other fish, crustaceans and insects.

Tropical Rainforest

The Amazon basin has a tropical climate — it is warm, humid and rainy all year round. This river basin supports the planet's largest rainforest, which is home to 40,000 plant species.

The Precious AMAZON RIVER

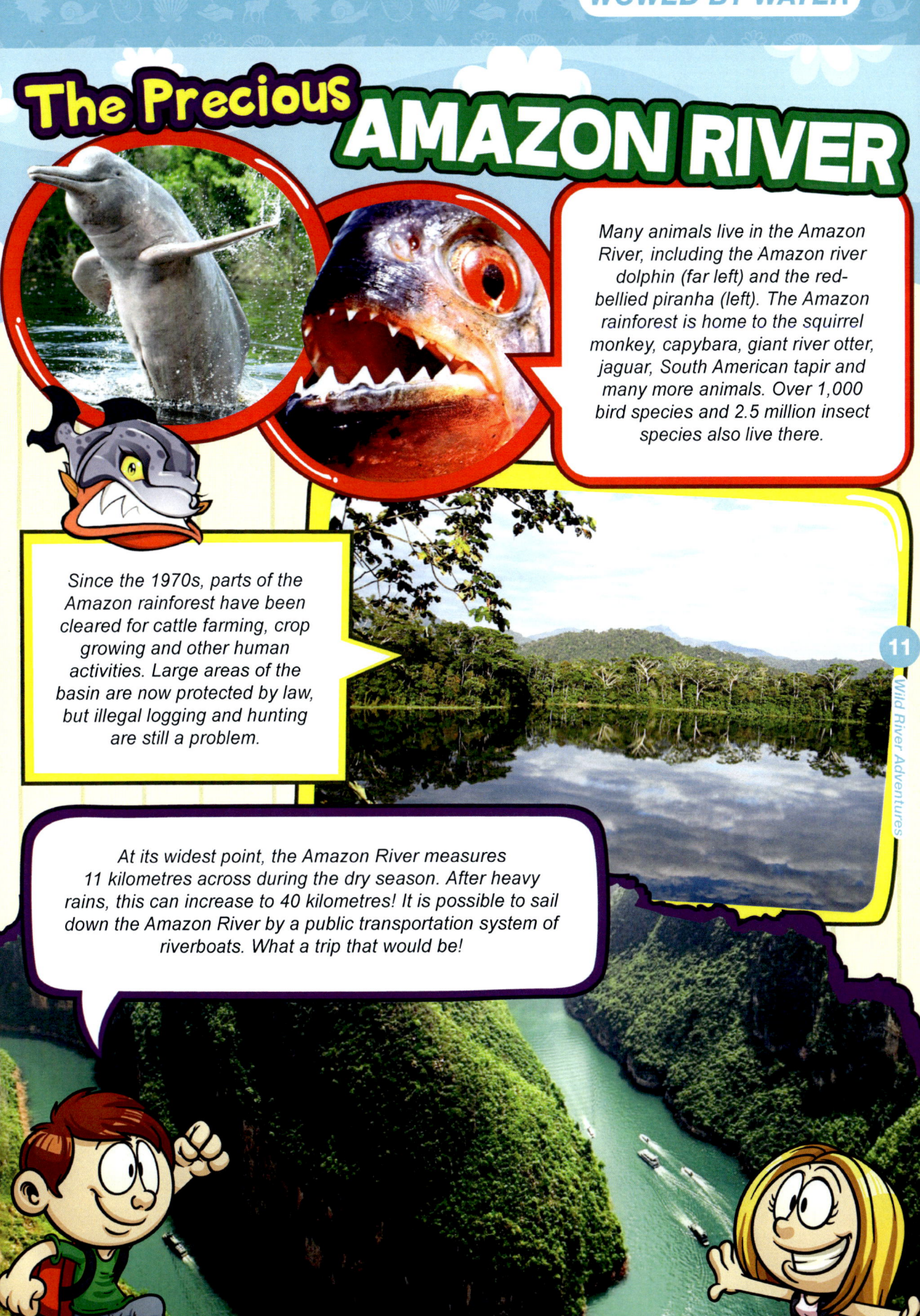

Many animals live in the Amazon River, including the Amazon river dolphin (far left) and the red-bellied piranha (left). The Amazon rainforest is home to the squirrel monkey, capybara, giant river otter, jaguar, South American tapir and many more animals. Over 1,000 bird species and 2.5 million insect species also live there.

Since the 1970s, parts of the Amazon rainforest have been cleared for cattle farming, crop growing and other human activities. Large areas of the basin are now protected by law, but illegal logging and hunting are still a problem.

At its widest point, the Amazon River measures 11 kilometres across during the dry season. After heavy rains, this can increase to 40 kilometres! It is possible to sail down the Amazon River by a public transportation system of riverboats. What a trip that would be!

11

Wild River Adventures

Falling... Falling...

Wakey, wakey! We're going to visit the Victoria Falls National Park today.

Well... I'm not going.

Okay, but Uncle Dennis arranged a helicopter for the trip...

Huh? I'm coming!

Me too!

At the Victoria Falls National Park, Zimbabwe...

I have our admission tickets. Shall we go?

Yahoo!

Let's go!

Chak-chak-chak...

That's our ride!

Yay...

Chak-chak-chak...

Wow!

Can you see that "smoke" rising in the distance? That's mist caused by the powerful currents of Victoria Falls as it cascades down.

It does look like smoke!

Now, below us is Devil's Pool, a natural rock pool at the edge of the waterfall.

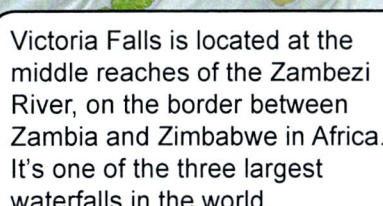

Look at the water sheet plunging a hundred metres down into the river.

Wow! I see the waterfall!

It looks out of this world!

Victoria Falls is located at the middle reaches of the Zambezi River, on the border between Zambia and Zimbabwe in Africa. It's one of the three largest waterfalls in the world.

Look, there's so much mist rising that sunlight is being refracted into rainbows!

13

Falling... Falling...

World Heritage Site

Victoria Falls is one of only about 200 natural sites worldwide listed by UNESCO (the United Nations Educational, Scientific and Cultural Organization) as areas of universal value, deserving protection so that future generations can enjoy them.

WOWED BY WATER

Local tribes call Victoria Falls "Mosi-oa-Tunya", which means "the smoke that thunders"!

Yes, the crashing waters are deafening!

Wow, a bridge spans the river gorge!

Yes, that bridge has a bungee-jumping facility.

Well, it's a 4-second freefall down a height of 111 metres — a real adrenaline rush!

That sounds very scary!

14

Falling... Falling...

Look at the river. It's so blue and crystal clear.

This is the Zambezi River, the fourth longest river in Africa and the longest river in southern Africa. Look closely, and you'll see elephants on the savannah.

On the way back to the helipad, upstream of the Zambezi River…

Dad, can we go up again?

Yeah, how about another ride, Dad?

No, I'm getting a little dizzy… I need to rest.

Border Crossing
Victoria Falls is on the border between Zimbabwe and Zambia. The Victoria Falls Bridge crosses the Zambezi River and connects the two countries. The 198-metre-long bridge carries a road, rail and footway.

Victoria Falls

Venezuela's Angel Falls is taller, and Khone Phapheng Falls in Laos is wider, but Victoria Falls has the distinction of being the world's largest waterfall, because of its height (108 metres) and width (1.7 kilometres) combined.

15

Falling... Falling...

Victoria Falls is part of the Mosi-oa-Tunya National Park of Zambia and the Victoria Falls National Park of Zimbabwe. These two parks are home to a wide variety of wildlife, including elephants, giraffes and Cape buffalo.

Around 2 million years ago, shifts in the Earth's plates changed the river patterns in central Zimbabwe, causing what is now the upper Zambezi River to flow over a steep drop, and join what is now the lower river. Thus, Victoria Falls was formed.

AR

Niagara Falls

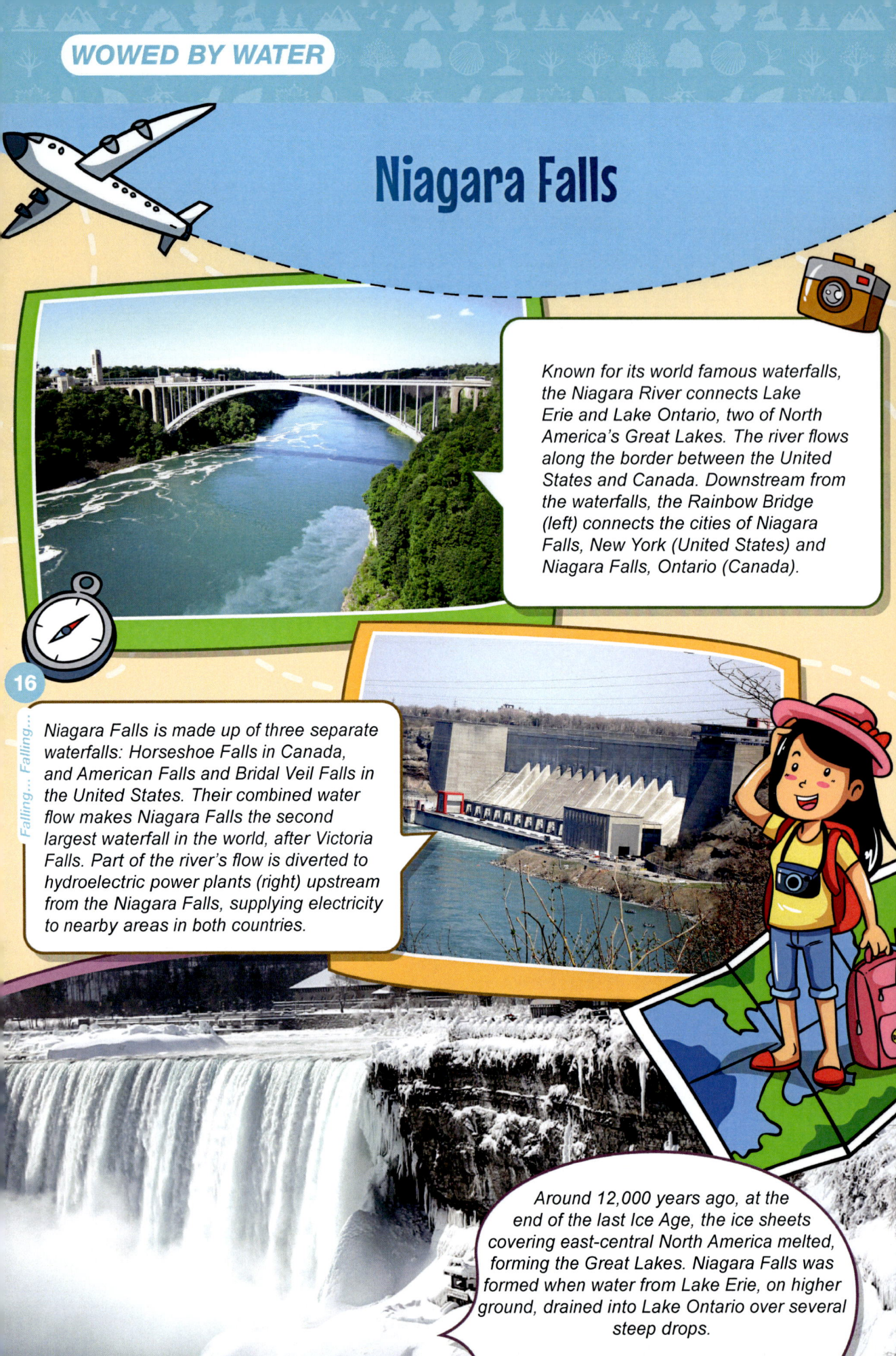

Known for its world famous waterfalls, the Niagara River connects Lake Erie and Lake Ontario, two of North America's Great Lakes. The river flows along the border between the United States and Canada. Downstream from the waterfalls, the Rainbow Bridge (left) connects the cities of Niagara Falls, New York (United States) and Niagara Falls, Ontario (Canada).

Falling... Falling...

16

Niagara Falls is made up of three separate waterfalls: Horseshoe Falls in Canada, and American Falls and Bridal Veil Falls in the United States. Their combined water flow makes Niagara Falls the second largest waterfall in the world, after Victoria Falls. Part of the river's flow is diverted to hydroelectric power plants (right) upstream from the Niagara Falls, supplying electricity to nearby areas in both countries.

Around 12,000 years ago, at the end of the last Ice Age, the ice sheets covering east-central North America melted, forming the Great Lakes. Niagara Falls was formed when water from Lake Erie, on higher ground, drained into Lake Ontario over several steep drops.

Ground of Many Colours

Island Nation

Mauritius consists of several islands in the Indian Ocean, about 2,000 kilometres off the southeastern coast of Africa, east of Madagascar. On the main island is an unusual mound of coloured sand covering an area of about 7,500 square metres (a little larger than a football pitch).

Charms of Chamarel

Chamarel, a small village in southwestern Mauritius, is home to the Seven Coloured Earth Geopark, a tortoise park, and the 100-metre tall Chamarel Waterfall. The village was founded more than 200 years ago and is a popular tourist destination today.

That's called Seven-Coloured Earth. It's a very special kind of soil found in Mauritius.

Geologists once mixed these different-coloured earths and put them in a tube. After a few days, the different colours separated from each other all on their own. It was amazing.

How do they separate from each other?

Well... Geologists are still investigating this at the moment. And that is why I'm here...

Benny, can you send another ten jars of it?

Why?

I want to give one to Mary, Judy, Rainee...

Oh no!

Volcanic Origins

The island of Mauritius was formed about 10 million years ago when a volcano erupted, spewing lava that cooled into basalt, a rock rich in iron, magnesium, aluminium and other metal compounds. At Chamarel, iron oxide has coloured the sands in red to brown shades, while aluminium oxide has produced shades ranging from blue to violet.

The Formation Of
SEVEN-COLOURED EARTH

The "dunes" at Chamarel's Seven Coloured Earth Geopark were formed by the gradual weathering of basalt, leaving iron and aluminium oxides that produce shades of red and blue respectively. The phenomenon was first noticed in the 1870s, and has been a popular tourist attraction since the 1960s.

The distinct colour bands show up best in morning sunlight. The patterns or rills in the sand are made by rainwater flowing across the landscape.

How does Seven Coloured Earth separate back into distinct colours after being mixed? Scientists are still trying to solve this mystery. The metal oxides may have some ability to repel each other, thus separating into layers.

21

New Mexico's White Desert

Urr?

Bobo!

Ah… You have ruined my sweet dream!

I didn't want to, but Mum asked me to wake you up.

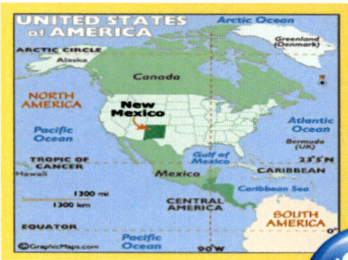

Ancient Dune Field

The white sands of Tularosa Basin, New Mexico, United States, have existed for at least 7,000 years. Covering more than 700 square kilometres (a little smaller than the land area of Singapore) and in places taller than a three-storey building, the dune field is visible from space.

Knowbot, is there a desert in the world where the sand is white?

Yes! White Sands National Park in the United States.

There is really such a place?

Yes, there is. Unlike other desert regions where the sand is somewhat yellow, White Sands is the real deal!

23

New Mexico's White Desert

Why do you suddenly ask about this place?

Because in my dream I was there, just playing in the white sand!

National Monument

White Sands was declared a national monument in 1934, after efforts to protect this area and its unique ecosystem were finally recognised by law.

No wonder you had a goofy smile on your face!

Ah…

The combination of white sands and clear blue skies is an enchanting sight and attracts a lot of visitors to White Sands National Monument.

But why would people go to a desert where it's so hot?

It's hot in summer during the day, but evenings are much cooler. In winter, there might even be frost or snow overnight. Besides, it's fun to surf in the sand!

I feel like going there to see for myself.

Me too!

White Sands Camouflage

Some 800 species of animals from all groups of the animal kingdom live in the white desert. Many have developed a lighter colouring than their relatives living outside the dunes. The greyish-white colour of the bleached earless lizard (left) is an adaptation to its white surroundings.

What are you doing?

I am going back to sleep. If I dream of White Sands National Monument, this time I'll be able to take some photographs with my camera.

Bobo, you are NOT going back to bed!

I was just kidding, Mum!

Ha ha ha...

Roads Through White Sands

According to archaeologists, ancient travellers took many trails and paths through White Sands, including wagon routes and a 19th-century Salt Trail left by the Spanish when they were mining salt. Today, the road to White Sands is Dunes Drive (right), located directly off Highway US-70 between the cities of Alamogordo and Las Cruces, New Mexico.

Why Is the Sand White?

The Tularosa Basin is surrounded by the San Andres and the Sacramento mountain ranges, which are made of layers of a clear mineral called gypsum. Gypsum is rarely found as sand because it is water soluble. However, because the basin has no outlet to the sea, dissolved gypsum remains there, where it is deposited by rainfall and snowmelt.

When water evaporates from the basin, it leaves behind selenite, the crystalline form of gypsum. Wind and water break down these crystals into progressively smaller and smaller particles, until they become fine grains of gypsum sand.

Gypsum sand appears white to the eye because the surfaces of each tiny particle reflect sunlight. Unlike normal (silica) sand, gypsum sand doesn't absorb the sun's heat. In summer it remains comfortable to walk on barefoot.

26

New Mexico's White Desert

Cappadocia's Stone Forest

Shortly after sunrise, at a launch site in Cappadocia, Turkey…

Uncle Phil, when is it our turn?

Be patient, Bobo!

Wow, multicoloured hot-air balloons are going up into the sky, one by one!

Why is it taking so long to inflate our balloon?

Strange Formations

Cappadocia occupies central Anatolia, in the heartland of Turkey. It is a semi-arid region with hot dry summers and cold snowy winters. The landscape is studded with mountains and volcanic rock formations of various shapes and sizes.

Well, high-pressured fans have to partially fill each balloon with cold air...

... and then, the air has to be heated until it creates enough lift for the basket and passengers.

I see! That must be the burner!

Yes, the hot air inside the balloon weighs less than the air outside it, enabling the balloon to float upwards.

Now, are you two ready for the experience of a lifetime?

Bring it on!

Bird's Eye View

Many of Cappadocia's towns and villages are nestled among rocky outcrops and weird, wonderful formations, making this region a popular destination for hot-air balloon tours.

Let's move out!

Wow! The rocks are very special!

The view is so beautiful. Let's take some souvenir snapshots.

Great!

Gee, where's Bobo?

Fairy Chimneys

Millions of years ago, volcanic eruptions covered Cappadocia in thick layers of ash that gradually hardened into a rock called tuff. Over time, wind and rain weathered away the softer rock, leaving mushroom-like pillars in the landscape. The tallest of these "fairy chimneys" are around 40 metres high.

Bobo, what's wrong with you?

I think I have acrophobia – I feel terrified whenever I look at the ground far below!

I'm sorry. The flight time of every hot-air balloon ride is fixed at an hour. We won't be able to set you down sooner.

What?

An hour later…

I was very scared, but this was a rare experience.

Ha ha!

Stone Housing

Cappadocia has been inhabited by people groups for thousands of years. To protect themselves against warring powers around them, the residents of Cappadocia began living in the stone — carving chambers and tunnel complexes into the soft rock to create multi-level towns extending underground.

Göreme National Park and the Rock Sites of Cappadocia have been a UNESCO World Heritage Site since 1985. Tourists from all over the world visit, to marvel at the way nature and human culture have come together to produce breathtaking structures.

Beautiful Cappadocia

In Pigeon Valley, near the town of Uçhisar, at the edge of Göreme National Park, people long ago lived in a network of caves carved into the cliff faces (left). The smaller holes housed pigeons, which were kept as message carriers.

The underground city of Derinkuyu (right), in Nevşehir Province, Cappadocia, is thought to have been built around 2,800 years ago. Consisting of more than 10 levels of corridors, chambers and smaller rooms, the city could hold at least 20,000 people. Air shafts opening above ground provided ventilation to all levels.

Walking with Giants

We can finally be together.

Uh… is there time to watch something else?

The plane is about to land. Please fasten your seatbelt.

Okay.

Coastal Marvel

Less than 100 kilometres from the city of Belfast, Northern Ireland, on the northern coast facing the Atlantic Ocean, a fascinating sight awaits the visitor. Tens of thousands of stone columns extend like a pathway out into sea!

We are finally here in Ireland!

Later we will visit one of Ireland's famous tourist attractions.

I'm going to take lots and lots of pictures later and show them to my classmates back home.

Myths and Legends

Stories abound regarding the origins of the stone formations known as Giant's Causeway. An Irish giant called Fionn mac Cumhaill (Finn McCool) is said to have built it to spar with a Scottish giant called Benandonner. Another version has it that Fionn built the causeway for love of a Scottish giantess.

This is Ireland's famous tourist attraction, Giant's Causeway.

Hey… this place looks a lot like the setting of the cartoon that I watched on the plane a while ago!

You were watching an animated movie about one of the legends surrounding Giant's Causeway!

In the cartoon, a giant built this land bridge.

I can see why storytellers would say that. Look at how neatly and closely these columns are arranged, with only a narrow space between them!

Walking with Giants

Mysterious Symmetry
Most of the stone columns at Giant's Causeway are hexagonal, or six-sided. However, columns with four, five, seven or eight sides also exist.

It's true! How unusual!

Those columns are uneven. They look like staircases!

How spectacular!

Standing on these stone columns, I feel like a giant.

It is an honour to see a view as beautiful as this with someone I love dearly. It makes this trip worthwhile.

Grandpa and Grandma sharing a romantic moment – ugh!

CRINGE!

Was It the Work of Giants?

Well, some great forces were certainly at work. About 50–60 million years ago, lava erupted through a crack in the Earth's crust, and hardened into a vast basalt plateau. As the rock cooled, it contracted, shrinking and cracking into thousands of columns. Wind and wave erosion carved the rock into its present form.

Giant's Causeway in County Antrim, Northern Ireland, is a 6-kilometre-long coastal rock formation made up of 40,000 interlocking natural basalt columns. It was named a UNESCO World Heritage Site in 1986.

Millions of years of wind and wave erosion have carved the columns into various heights and formations. Most are nestled together like staircases. The tallest columns stand at a height of more than 12 metres.

37

Walking with Giants

Erosion has also created other basalt formations within this area. One resembles a huge boot, another a camel, inspiring more tales about the exploits of Fionn mac Cumhaill, the Irish giant.

World's Biggest Cat

At a research sanctuary for rare animals…

Hey… that is no ordinary tiger…

A naturalist like you might be interested in our special resident!

Is it safe for me to be near it?

Let me introduce Samson, the liger, the offspring of a male lion and female tiger. He is a gentle beast.

Gentle? Are you sure?

Hungry Carnivore

The liger is an enormous animal that has the colour of a lion, with faint stripes. Standing on its hind legs, an adult can reach 3.5 metres in height. It eats an average of about 10 kilograms of meat a day. This is more than either a lion or tiger, which typically eats less than 8 kilograms a day.

We have raised him from a cub — he is very used to being around humans.

How heavy is this fellow?

Samson currently weighs about 400 kilograms.

Wow, how long is he when he stretches his body out?

You can see for yourself, when we feed him later!

I look forward to that!

Samson's meal arrives in a bucket…

This is what Samson eats?

Yes, mainly cattle meat, chicken meat and eggs.

In a moment Gina will feed him from a 4-metre-high stand.

Wow, I have to see this.

Hear Me Roar!
Ligers make sounds like both tigers and lions, but their roar sounds more like that of lions. However, they seem to inherit the tiger's love of swimming.

He easily reaches the platform when he stands on his hind legs!

You didn't expect that, did you?

Why is a liger so big?

It has to do with its genes.

The liger is the offspring of two animals from the same genus, or family group, but different species.

A kind of hybrid?

Yes. Male lion genes encourage size growth. Normally, these genes are balanced out by female lion genes, but tiger genes lack the ability to discourage size growth.

I see! So a male lion paired with a female tiger produces a giant!

Exactly. Like Samson here!

Big Baby

Because of the liger's huge size, the tiger mother can have difficulty giving birth. A caesarean section (an operation that cuts through the mother's abdominal wall) may be necessary to deliver her cub.

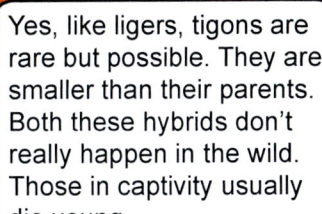

Can female lions have offspring with male tigers?

Yes, like ligers, tigons are rare but possible. They are smaller than their parents. Both these hybrids don't really happen in the wild. Those in captivity usually die young.

Why?

As distinct species, lions and tigers wouldn't normally mate. Their offspring tend to have genetic defects and health problems.

Laws should make it illegal to breed such hybrids.

Animal rights groups are working to put such laws in place. We rescued Samson from breeders who would have charged money for people to view him.

Den, come join us for a group photo!

Is it safe?

You have nothing to fear.

Race to the Finish

The cheetah wins hands — or paws — down, of course. But the liger can match the tiger for speed, and easily outruns a human being.

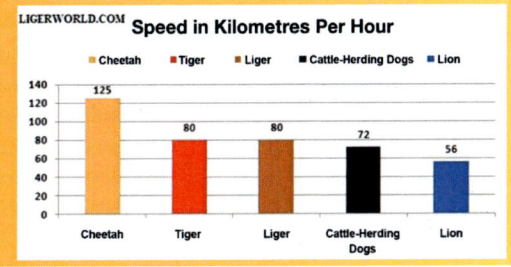

LIGERWORLD.COM **Speed in Kilometres Per Hour**

Cheetah · Tiger · Liger · Cattle-Herding Dogs · Lion

	Cheetah	Tiger	Liger	Cattle-Herding Dogs	Lion
Speed	125	80	80	72	56

The world's largest cat

Both lions and tigers belong to the family of big cats, but they do not share the same habitats in the wild. Hybrid offspring are the accidental or planned result of humans keeping the two species together in captivity. Most experts consider this breeding practice unethical and irresponsible, because the offspring are prone to genetic defects.

Heaviest liger

According to the Guinness Book of Records, the world's largest living big cat is Hercules, a liger weighing 418 kilograms and measuring 3.3 metres from head to tail. Born in 2002, Hercules lives at Myrtle Beach Safari Wildlife preserve in South Carolina, United States.

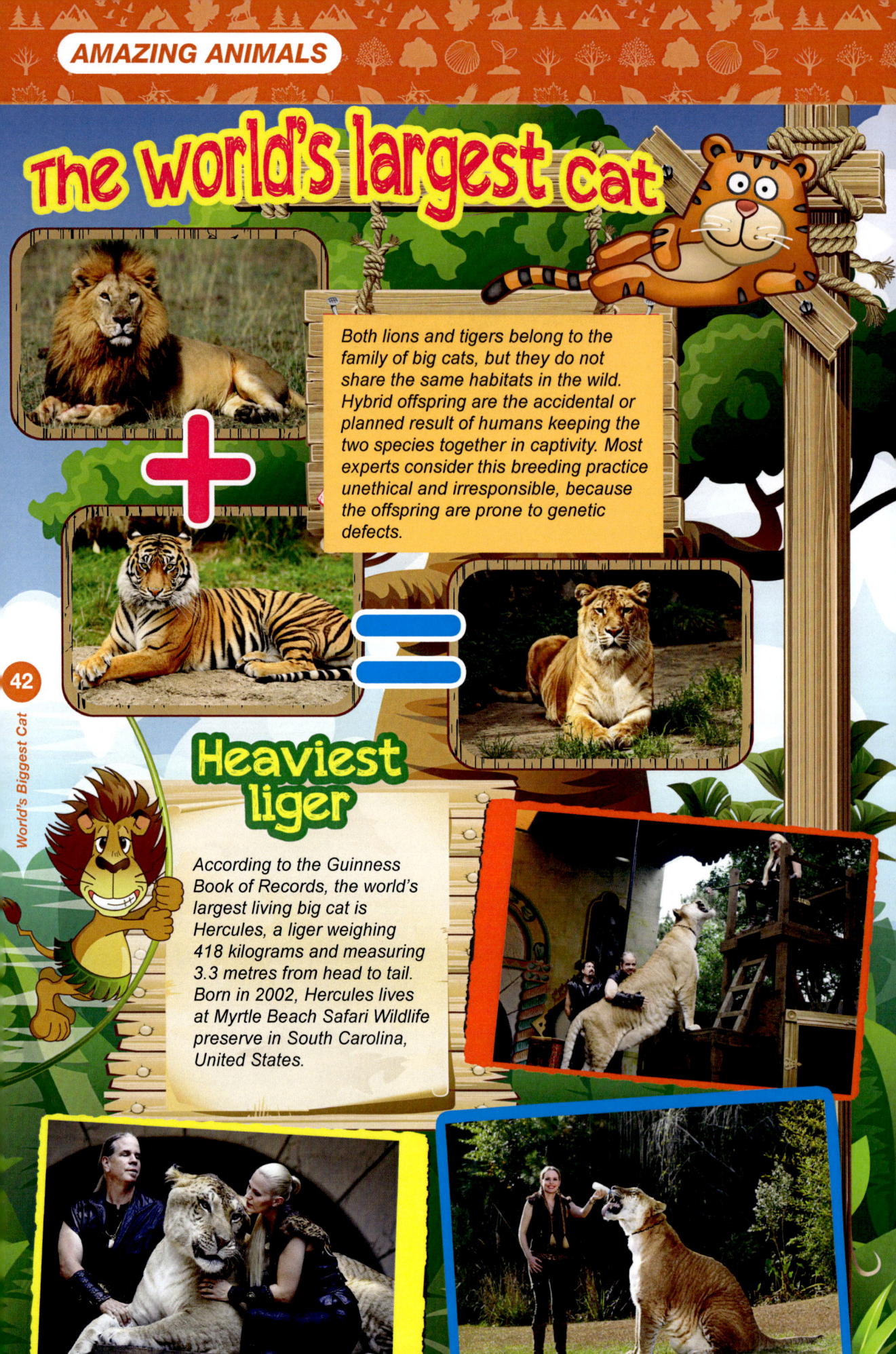

What a Strange Fish!

In the sea off Bali island, Indonesia…

I'm so excited!

So am I!

Ha ha… you guys always start off thrilled and then get nervous in the water. Check if you've got all your diving gear ready.

Is… is that a shark?

What do we do? I don't want to be shark food, Den!

Right! Den, we'd better go back!

Den, what's wrong? Why do you all look so serious and scared?

Eric, look! Here comes a shark!

Oh, don't worry. That's not a shark.

But what about that fin sticking out of the water!

Eric, if it's not a shark, what is it?

Relax, it's not a shark. It's an ocean sunfish.

Ocean sunfish?

Yes. When an ocean sunfish comes up to the surface, its large dorsal fin can be easily mistaken for a shark's.

Are ocean sunfish as dangerous as sharks?

No, they aren't. Ocean sunfish are huge, but they are gentle by nature and do not attack people.

Scientists haven't discovered much about them yet, and few people get to see them up close, so you'd better seize this opportunity.

When we're diving with the sunfish, is there anything we shouldn't do?

What a Strange Fish!

Half a Fish?

The ocean sunfish (*Mola mola*), also known as the common mola, has rough, thick, scaleless skin. It has an odd shape — its tail fin never grows into a tail but instead becomes a lumpy structure called a clavus. The clavus extends from the dorsal (top) fin to the anal (bottom) fin, and functions like a rudder, helping the sunfish steer itself.

Don't touch or feed the sunfish. And don't swim behind it because this will frighten it.

Okay! Let's dive now. I really want to see what an ocean sunfish really looks like.

Half an hour later...

We were right beside a sunfish — what an amazing experience!

Right! It was such a big one. But it did look weird. And it was swimming very slowly.

It's a clumsy swimmer. It spends most of its time diving in the depths to feed, but it rises to the surface to warm itself.

That's when its dorsal fin fooled us. Ha ha!

Good Catch!

Ocean sunfish face predators such as sharks, killer whales and sea lions. California sea lions have been known to tear the fins off sunfish and toss them about like frisbees, without always eating them!

45

What a Strange Fish!

What do ocean sunfish feed on?

Their main food is jellyfish, but they also eat small fish, crustaceans, squid, algae and tiny water organisms called zooplankton.

In turn, until they get too big to be eaten, their slowness makes them easy prey for sharks or killer whales.

So, is the ocean sunfish an endangered species?

Well, it does have one powerful survival technique — a female sunfish can lay about 300 million eggs at a time!

It's really unimaginable!

That's a lot!

So, the sunfish population should be huge, right?

Not necessarily. Sunfish eggs are fertilised externally, so unless a male sunfish releases its sperm nearby, many of the eggs never hatch.

Even if the eggs hatch, sunfish young, or fry, easily fall prey to larger fish such as bluefin tuna and dolphinfish.

Deep Sea Diver
The ocean sunfish spends a lot of time seeking out jellyfish at depths of 600 metres or more. In some areas, they easily dive down to the seafloor.

What a Strange Fish!

Eric, why don't we see more ocean sunfish in aquariums?

Because they grow to a huge size, ocean sunfish can only be housed in the biggest marine aquariums.

I see.

You can admire them in Monterey Bay Aquarium in California, United States, or Kaiyukan Aquarium in Osaka, Japan, or...

Krool~~

I wasn't really talking about seafood, but it sounds like someone's hungry!

Ha ha ha! Let's head back to shore, then!

Vulnerable to Humans

Scientists suspect that ocean sunfish populations may be dwindling. In some countries, ocean sunfish are considered delicacies and fished for their flesh. They are also killed when they become tangled in fishing nets (right) or when they swallow plastic bags, mistaking them for jellyfish.

The Ocean Sunfish

The ocean sunfish is the world's largest bony fish. It lives in temperate and tropical seas around the world. It can grow up to a length of 3 metres from head to clavus, and 4 metres from dorsal fin to anal fin. Mature specimens can weigh 2,000 kilograms or more!

48

What a Strange Fish!

As many as 40 kinds of parasites can infest the skin of an ocean sunfish. It may try to get rid of them by leaping out of and back into the water. It also gets help from seabirds, allowing them to pick the parasites off its plate-like body. What a feast!

Ocean sunfish reproduce by broadcast spawning. This means that the female releases eggs into the water. At around the same time, the male releases sperm to fertilise the eggs. Ocean sunfish fry (left) measure only about 2 millimetres across, and are covered with tiny spines that disappear as they grow up.

Log Cakes in the Snow

On a snowy evening in winter…

Yeah! We've finished our snowman!

Whoosh...

Brr… Knowbot, it is getting windier… brr… and colder. Let's go home now. Brr…

Okay, Bobo!

We'll come back to build another snowman tomorrow!

Okay!

49

Whoosh...
Whoosh...

The next morning…

Come on, Knowbot, hurry up!

Coming!

Huh?

What are these? How did they get here?

Huh?

Hmm… They weren't here yesterday!

Hmm… Someone must have made them last night.

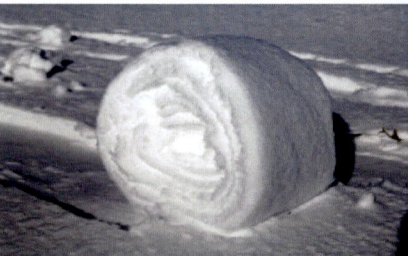

Nature's "Cake Rolls"

A snow roller is a snowdrift that is formed by the wind. It is usually cylindrical in shape and looks like a cake roll. Snow rollers are formed in wintry, windy conditions, mostly in North America or northern Europe.

Huh? But I don't see any footprints…

What if… they were made by space aliens?!

Huh?

Ha ha ha...

Ahhh...

Ahhh...

Bobo, you have a wild imagination! These were not made by aliens.

Then, you did these?

Ha ha, of course not! I can't even talk — you're only imagining it!

51

Log Cakes in the Snow

Picked Up by the Wind

Snow rollers are a rare occurrence. When snow falls thickly on flat, open ground or a gently sloping plain, strong winds can peel off the top layer of snow, forming a roll that gathers more layers as it is blown along by the wind.

What exactly are these? How did they form?

They are called snow rollers.

Snow rollers?

Snow rollers are the masterworks of nature.

Oh!

Oh!

Masterworks of nature? How?

I've got it! It was windy last night. It must have been the wind that rolled up the snow!

Rolls and Doughnuts

Snow rollers range in size — they can be as small as tennis balls or more than half a metre across. Most are hollow, because the ice layers in the centre are thinnest and get blown away as the roll grows.

Actually, there must be four essential conditions for snow rollers to form.

What are the four conditions?

They are temperature, humidity, wind speed and terrain.

Yes, it must be cold enough to snow. Yet the top layer of snow must melt just enough to be peeled off by wind that is strong enough to blow across flat or gently sloping ground.

Hurray, Knowbot, we solved the mystery!

Say "cheese"!

53

Log Cakes in the Snow

Now You Know!
Every few winters or so, snow rollers appear on the prairies of southern Idaho in the United States. They can stand about half a metre tall!

Marshmallows in the Sky

Bobo and Knowbot are having a picnic at the park…

Oh, I am very hungry now. I'll look for food here!

Great, I see some picnickers on the ground! I'll find something to eat there!

Scream…

Huh? Those clouds are unusual!

This looks puzzling! Maybe the weather is going to change…

Scream...

How do you like the sandwiches I made, Knowbot?

I can't wait to try one, Bobo.

Aaah!

Pomp!

Aaah!

Huh? How could an eagle fall from the sky?

Huh?

Stormy Weather Warning

Have you ever seen blobs like these in the sky? Mammatus clouds look like lumpy protrusions on the undersides of regular clouds. They are associated with stormy weather, appearing before or after a thunderstorm or a hail storm.

Something up there scared me, and I lost my balance.

What frightened you?

Those clouds! Don't you think they look weird and creepy?

Huh? **Huh?**

Hmm... Those clouds look like marshmallows!

I've never seen clouds like these. Could they mean the end of the world?

End of the world?

Marshmallows in the Sky

How Are Mammatus Clouds Formed?

When tiny water droplets from a cloud layer move into dry air below and evaporate, the air is cooled, sinking to form pouch-like sacs made up mainly of ice particles. Mammatus clouds can extend across the sky for hundreds of kilometres.

Does anything happen when these clouds appear?

No! They are mammatus clouds. They form when a cloud layer mixes with warmer, drier air below.

Sometimes, but not always.

Some people think mammatus clouds accompany storms, but this isn't always true.

Oh well, at least we get to see these unusual clouds. Are you less frightened now, Eagle?

Yes, in fact, the clouds look rather beautiful reflecting the colours of sunset!

Now You See Them...

Mammatus clouds remain visible until the ice particles that form them evaporate. If the sinking air contains large droplets and snow crystals, the clouds remain visible longer, because larger particles require greater amounts of energy to evaporate.

Rare Occurrence

Count yourself fortunate if you spot mammatus clouds — they are among the rarest of cloud formations and seldom remain visible for more than 15 minutes.

World's Largest Salt Pan

At a very special hotel in Bolivia…

We are staying here for the night.

This is your room. Please make yourselves at home.

This bed is awesome!

Please do not lick the walls!

Hah?

What's a Salt Pan?

Natural salt pans are expanses of flat ground covered with salt and other minerals. Salar de Uyuni is the world's largest salt flat, with an area of 10,582 square kilometres — that's the size of more than 2 million football fields! It is located in southwestern Bolivia, more than 3,500 metres above sea level.

World's Largest Salt Pan

Why would anyone want to lick the walls?

Please do not lick the walls!

It's because this hotel is made of salt. Everything — from the tables and chairs, to the pillars and bed cabinets — is made of salt!

Hah?

Some hotel guests lick the walls to find out whether it's true. The hotel owner has politely requested that we not do that, to prevent the walls from getting thinner. Licking anything in the room would be very unhygienic, anyway.

I don't care — I want to taste the walls!

Not a chance, girls. It's bedtime, anyway.

Right, because tomorrow we will set off on a special journey.

When the Water Evaporated

Salar de Uyuni roughly means "enclosed salt flat" in Spanish. It was formed by the drying up of a large lake that covered the region more than 30,000 years ago. A crust of salt several metres thick was left behind.

Where will we be going tomorrow?

We're going to visit the largest salt flat in the world.

So, there's nothing there but salt?

Is it the kind of salt we eat every day?

You will have to wait till tomorrow to see for yourselves.

How am I supposed to go to sleep when they haven't answered any of our questions?

Aw, they didn't want to spoil the fun of discovery. Get some sleep!

From the Desert to the Dining Table

Salar de Uyuni contains an estimated 10 billion tonnes of salt. Every year, less than 25,000 tonnes are extracted. Before the salt becomes edible or used in food seasoning, it is processed to remove other minerals and impurities.

The next day…

We're almost there.

Wow! This is an incredible place. The ground looks like a mirror reflecting the sky!

We are at Salar de Uyuni, the world's largest salt flat.

I can't wait to get down and taste the salt!

Wow, the land is so white, and so flat!

From the bus, at a distance, the ground looked like it was covered in ice. But now I can feel the salt in my hands.

Salt Desert Ecosystem

Little wildlife or vegetation lives on the salt pan, but it is home to giant cacti that reach a height of 12 metres. Salar de Uyuni is also the breeding ground for three species of pink South American flamingos: the Chilean, Andean, and rare James' flamingos.

Yucks, this is very salty.

Ha ha ha...

Come with me — let's take some photos on the other side.

Girls, don't stray too far. It's easy to lose your sense of direction and location, when everything around you is all white.

World's Largest Salt Pan

In that case, let's just stay here. Ready, smile...

Not Just Salt

The Bolivian government is excited about Salar de Uyumi's store of lithium, believed to be about 15 percent of the world's supply. Lithium is experiencing growing demand as a component of electric car batteries.

Salar de Uyuni

The part of the Andes Mountains where Salar de Uyuni is located has a relatively stable average temperature, with a daytime high of 21 degrees Celsius in summer, and a low of 13 degrees Celsius in winter. Nights are cold all year round, with temperatures between -9 and 5 degrees Celsius.

There is little rainfall in this region, but during the wet season from December to April, rainwater collects in the salt pan, forming a vast lake.

During the dry season from April to November, the surface of the salt pan hardens and contracts, cracking into hexagonal (six-sided) "tiles" that extend as far as the eye can see.

When the salt pan becomes a lake after the rains, it reflects the clouds and skies above like a mirror, so that it can be hard to tell where the lake ends and the sky begins.

Africa's Tallest Mountain

In the Amboseli National Park, Kenya…

The zebras are beside us!

There are some leopards resting on that tree branch.

Wow! I get to see so many wild animals here. It's such a rare experience!

What's that tall mountain in the distance?

That's Mount Kilimanjaro.

I'm going to open the roof of the car, so that we can admire the scenery better.

Yes, but first, we have to cross the border into Tanzania and enter Mount Kilimanjaro National Park.

Is that Africa's highest peak? Aren't we going to climb that?

How was Mount Kilimanjaro formed?

About 25 million years ago, crustal faults made a great rift valley in East Africa.

Due to a large-scale uplift of the crust, and violent magma flows, a series of volcanoes, including Mount Kilimanjaro, formed on both sides of the rift valley.

Mt. Kilimanjaro

Sleeping Volcano

Mount Kilimanjaro is located in Tanzania, close to the border with Kenya, on the eastern coast of the continent of Africa. It is a snowcapped volcano that last erupted around 360,000 years ago. Scientists think it could erupt again some time in the future.

Is there a crater at the top of the mountain?

Kilimanjaro actually has three peaks. The highest, Kibo, has a crater measuring 2.4 kilometres across and about 200 metres deep.

Is that snow on the mountain?

Yes! The top of the mountain is covered by snow all year round.

Because of global warming, the glaciers have been shrinking.

I hope the glaciers stop melting.

67

Africa's Tallest Mountain

This view is spectacular!

Three Peaks

Mount Kilimanjaro consists of three volcanic cones: Shira (3,962 metres), Mawenzi (5,149 metres) and Kibo (5,895 metres). Shira and Mawenzi are extinct — they will never erupt again.

Mawenzi
16,893 ft /5,149m

Kibo
19,341 ft / 5,895m

Shira
13,000 ft/ 3,962m

Africa's Tallest Mountain

A few days later...

We've reached the mountaintop!

Yay! Kibo, the highest peak of Mount Kilimanjaro.

We are standing on one of the world's tallest mountains. The only peaks higher than this are Mount Denali in Alaska, Mount Aconcagua in Argentina, and Mount Everest in the Himalayas.

Let's take some pictures.

Later...

I climbed Africa's tallest mountain!

You're awesome!

Melting Ice

Despite Mount Kilimanjaro's location in the tropics, the glaciers and ice fields on its summit have been in place for at least 11,000 years. It is predicted, however, that they will be gone by the year 2050, due to climate change.

Mount Kilimanjaro

Mount Kilimanjaro lies just 3 degrees south of the Equator, at the centre of Mount Kilimanjaro National Park. The area became a UNESCO World Heritage Site in 1987.

Africa's Tallest Mountain

Ascending Mount Kilimanjaro would take us through many climate zones, beginning with bushland and farmland on the lower slopes. Above the rainforest line, the landscape is dominated by heather moorland (right).

Above 4,000 metres, we would trek through a cold highland desert (left), followed by a frozen Arctic zone at the summit.

Glowing Waters

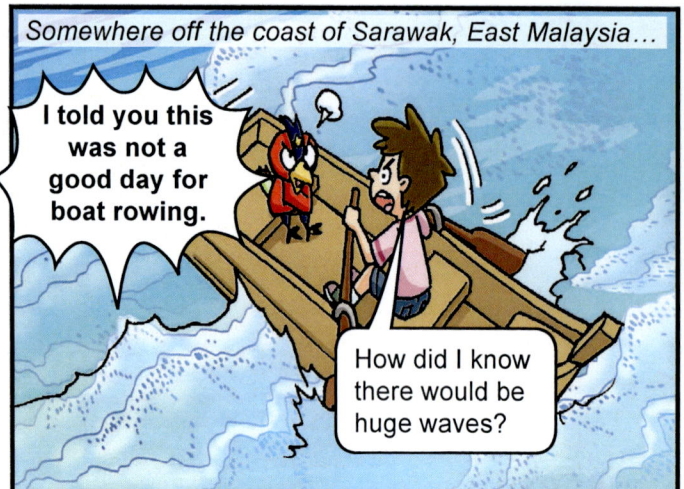

Somewhere off the coast of Sarawak, East Malaysia…

I told you this was not a good day for boat rowing.

How did I know there would be huge waves?

Oh no!

What's that?

A gigantic wave is going to capsize our boat!

Splash!

He's pretty heavy! I can't hold him with my own strength.

Suddenly...

Do you need help?

Come on, the shore is nearby...

Okay!

Ryan is taken safely to shore...

Are you alright?

A... a turtle?

Wow, what are all those tiny lights on the beach? They're beautiful...

Your boat capsized, and you almost drowned...

Good thing Turtle found and rescued you, Ryan!

Tidal Lights

Many tiny organisms called plankton live and float near the surface of the sea. Some produce light through a chemical reaction in their cells, a process known as bioluminescence.

This is Tusan Beach. It's not the beach that emits light, it's the bioluminescent microorganisms that live in the sea.

How do they emit light?

They produce a bluish glow by means of a chemical reaction in their cells.

These organisms can be bacteria, algae, jellyfish or insects. The blue light in different light-emitting seas can be caused by different bioluminescent microorganisms.

Why do they emit light?

It's how they communicate, attract mates, catch prey or scare predators away.

But bioluminescence isn't a very commonly observed phenomenon.

Why is that?

See the Sparkles?

The waters around Taiwan's Matsu Islands (left) are home to *Noctiluca scintillans*, a single-celled marine microorganism that exhibits bioluminescence when disturbed. Also known as the sea sparkle, this organism is the cause of the Blue Tears phenomenon — the beautiful glow that draws tourists to these islands.

Well, bioluminescent organisms are harder to spot if the seawater is polluted or murky, or if the glow is obstructed by landforms.

And humans are destroying many of the natural habitats of bioluminescent organisms.

People are becoming more aware of Earth's environmental problems. Hopefully, the situation will improve!

Ryan!

I hope so.

It's Mum and Dad!

I was so worried about you!

It won't happen again.

Fire in Their Bellies

Fireflies light up because of a chemical reaction inside their abdomens. A firefly can "switch" its light on or off by controlling the amount of oxygen added to the other chemicals needed to produce light. Firefly bioluminescence does not harm the firefly because it does not produce much heat.

Glowing Waters

Mudhdhoo Island

The microorganisms in the sea around Mudhdhoo Island in the Maldives wash up on the beach from time to time, covering whole stretches of sand with dots of blue light.

Luminous Lagoon

The warm, shallow waters of Luminous Lagoon in Jamaica provide ideal conditions for dinoflagellates (single-celled bioluminescent organisms) to thrive.

Toyama Beach

Every year, from March to June, firefly squid rise from the depths of Japan's Toyama Bay in search of mates. Tens of thousands of them together create a spectacular electric-blue lightshow on Toyoma Beach.

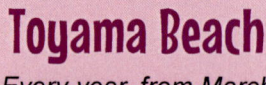

Star Attractions

Isn't this a limestone cave? And limestone is mainly calcium carbonate, which doesn't dissolve in water.

Well...

Actually, Manny is right. When rainwater becomes weak acid water, it is able to dissolve calcium carbonate.

How does weak acid water form?

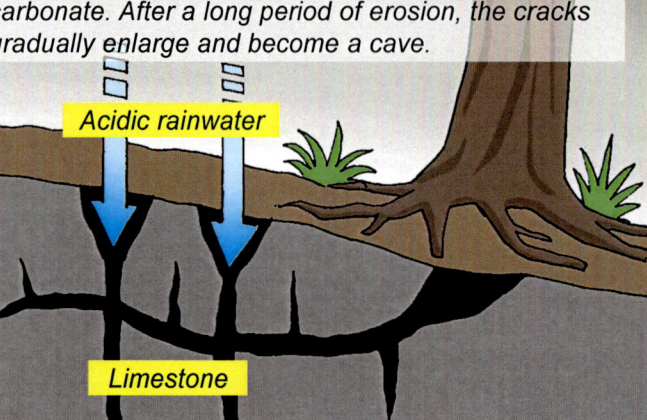

When rain falls, it meets with carbon dioxide in the air and soil and becomes weak acid water. This penetrates limestone cracks and dissolves calcium carbonate. After a long period of erosion, the cracks gradually enlarge and become a cave.

Acidic rainwater

Limestone

Haha, now I understand!

It's never too late to learn!

Oh, is it getting even darker in here?

Yes!

Get ready to see something spectacular soon!

Oh, wow, it's so beautiful!

It's magical!

Hidden Wonder Revealed

Shown here is the exit from the Waitomo Glowworm Caves, located in southern Waikato on New Zealand's North Island. These caves were originally underwater, rising to the surface after long periods of volcanic activity and movement in the Earth's crust.

Don't touch!

Huh?

Are they dangerous?

Dave, are those lights from fireflies?

No, they're glowworms. They're the larvae of a species of gnat called *Arachnocampa luminosa*, which is unique to New Zealand.

How could they be dangerous?

No, they can't hurt us, but the glowworms are sensitive to light and disturbance. If they're touched, they hide and stop giving off light.

Oh, that would be a pity.

Do you see the dangling threads produced by the glowworms?

Wow! Those are beautiful traps!

Kind of like spidersilk, huh? You don't want to get it all over your hands!

They're sticky silk traps. The glowworms emit a weak light to attract insects into the caves. Insects that come into contact with the silk threads get stuck and become glowworm food.

Slow Geological Processes

Limestone is a rock made up of calcium carbonate and other minerals. Most limestone is formed by fossil corals, shells and fish bone. These deposits collect in layers on the seafloor. They are broken down, mixed with minerals and compressed into rock by the weight of the water over millions of years.

More importantly, if their lights go out, won't the glowworms have no insects to eat?

That's right. This species is found in dense woodland and caves all over the world, but human activity threatens its survival.

If these gnats become extinct, these caves will lose their special appeal.

We must protect the New Zealand glowworm!

Sshhh... not so loud!

Oh!

Manny can be so embarrassing!

Responsible Tourism

Visitors to the Waitomo Glowworm Caves are not permitted to touch the limestone formations, use flash photography or smoke. These regulations protect the cave environment and preserve it as a natural wonder.

Sediments In Limestone Caves

Limestone caves, also known as karst caves, are formed by erosion over a long period of time. Rainwater or underground water mixes with carbon dioxide in the air, forming a weak acid that dissolves calcium carbonate.

When stalactite water drips constantly onto the cave floor, calcium carbonate deposits slowly "grow" from the bottom up. These are called stalagmites.

When weak acid containing dissolved calcium carbonate drips from cave ceilings, the mineral is deposited in needle-like formations extending downward. These are called stalactites.

When a stalactite keeps growing and a stalagmite constantly projects upwards, both these two sedimentary structures join together and form a column.

79

Star Attractions

So, How Much Do You Really Know About Natural Wonders?

Challenge yourself to recall key moments of your Adventures with Natural Wonders, and find out where you rank on the Geology Stack!

Get ready, get set, scan!

GEOLOGY STACK!	
10	**Everest Mountaineer! Congratulations, we're impressed!**
9–8	**Tablelands Trekker! Great job!**
7–6	**Highlander! Do even better next time!**
5–4	**Rope Climber! Get the hang of it and try again!**
3–0	**Rock Bottom! Try again!**

80

What is a matamata?
Why do wildebeest migrate?
Where can you find "fairy chimneys"?
Who discovered colour-blindness?
How does a lie detector work?

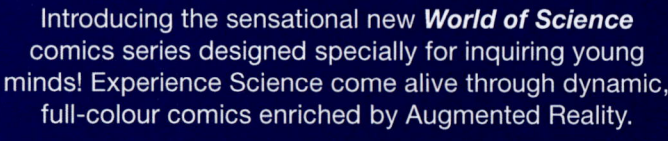

Introducing the sensational new *World of Science* comics series designed specially for inquiring young minds! Experience Science come alive through dynamic, full-colour comics enriched by Augmented Reality.

Books in this series so far:
Birds
Plants and Fungi
Insects
Aquatic Creatures
Human Body
Land Animals
Reptiles and Amphibians
Natural Wonders
How Things Work
Great Minds

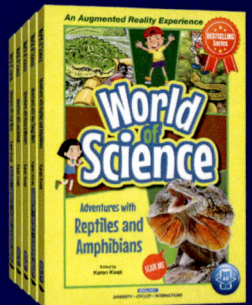

Look out for *Tech and Gadgets*, *Green Movement*, *Germs and Your Health*, *Materials*, *More Land Animals*, and many more!

To receive updates about children's titles from WS Education,
go to **https://www.worldscientific.com/page/newsletter/subscribe**, choose "**Education**",
click on "**Children's Books**" and key in your email address.